Out of **DARKNESS**
Into the *Light*

DAVID WONDERLICH

ISBN 978-1-63874-684-3 (paperback)
ISBN 978-1-63874-685-0 (digital)

Christian Faith Publishing
832 Park Avenue
Meadville, PA 16335
www.christianfaithpublishing.com

Printed in the United States of America

PREFACE

Some of my earliest recollections were of my father working while I was at home with my mother who was bedridden with doctor's orders. She was pregnant and needed to rest. I would ask for her company, and she usually replied, "Just go pray." I did just that. I believe the time I spent lying down on the rug in my bedroom, talking in prayer, was the beginning of a lifelong relationship with the Spirit that is within and the Lord of the world. I believe I was conscious of the relationship cemented in prayer. The canoe accident was one more step in the formation of myself and my individual consciousness. I firmly believe that the more conscious we are, the more attuned we become to the Spirit which is in all of us. Then, we can begin to transcend the trappings of the material and the conventional in everyday life.

ACKNOWLEDGMENTS

Pennsylvania Fish and Boat Commission. Not long after the canoe accident, the Pennsylvania Fish Commission (that would later change to the Pennsylvania Fish and Boat Commission) focused on conversations concerning a law that would require personal flotation devices (PFDs) for each person in nonmotorized, manual watercraft. This was passed, and I am sure the new law has saved many lives and much heartache over the years.

Josephine Casale. My mother's mother was such a motivation for writing. She was very sick, and I believe her will to live came from her need to write and get onto paper what was living in her mind. She talked almost daily to me about what she needed to say, and her story gave her the power and strength to survive. After being told she had only a few months to live, she completed her book almost two years later! Her husband, my grandfather, was my partner in the wild. He took me to the woods, lakes, and streams from my earliest years all the way to his passing. He and my grandmother live inside me.

Martha Wool. My great aunt was my grandmother Josephine's sister. To me, Aunt Martha had the most creative mind, and I appreciated visiting her whenever possible. She took our conversations well beyond the normal, and showed me that everyday life could be expanded beyond the everyday. She was a gifted human, well ahead of her time. I do miss her so much!

Arthur Wonderlich. My grandfather on my father's side is an inspiration because he worked his entire life to invent the machinery he dreamed of. His father, David, was a pioneer in Nebraska and gave his son his "explore gene." His fertile mind had almost no limits, especially with my grandmother by his side. I still have one of his original patents!

W. Scott Yoder. My incredible friend, Scott, is a retired English teacher and fly fisherman; we always have a lot to talk about. He has read my magazine articles over the years and couldn't wait for the story of Dan, the canoe accident, and the kids I taught. Scott gave so much advice and support along the way! Scott and our conversations helped make it possible to complete what had been started so long ago!

Kathy Novak. Kathy is such an amazing friend. At the campground where we have campers, we discovered our love of talking about and sharing ideas on religion, politics, philosophy, the outdoors, nature, beauty, and just about anything else that is stimulated by our campfires! Kathy had so many ideas along the way, which helped my writing of this book materialize. She ran out of her camper one day and said, "The Spirit gave me the perfect title. It should be called *Out of Darkness Into the Light.*" And she, once again, got it right!

Rachael Wonderlich. My youngest daughter, Rachael, knew I was writing this book and asked to read what I had. She took the book and got all the meaning from it, which I had meant for it to have in her first reading. We are related! Rachael has been a motivation to keep the book the way it came from my soul. Rachael and Elizabeth, daughters, along with John and David, sons, have given me wonderful support all their lives.

Marjorie Wonderlich. My wife had to struggle along with me and my labors in getting this book "right." It wasn't always easy as it took many, many years. Marge was there to reassure me while asking hard questions to help me maintain focus. She was tireless as the years went by and always gave me confidence that I would succeed in telling the story the way it should be told. Thank you!

God. It was God whom I had the final conversation with on the upside-down, partially submerged canoe that late afternoon in February many years ago. God was there when I was three, and I spent time each day talking with him, and he was not only there every day, but he was certainly present when I asked for his help on that canoe to make it to shore. It was a long journey to safety, but as clearly as I was lifted up from the water, he was there every barefoot, snowy step back to civilization. Again, thank you, God.

The twenty-seventh of February opened with a bright sky and a weather report that looked more like late May than the typical white, cold of mid-February. Temperatures were to reach well into the sixties, and most minds turned to spring. It became the kind of day when people were outside walking, washing their cars in short-sleeved shirts, enjoying the sun and warmth, and I was no different.

I called Dan and said, "Why don't we go up Little Pine Creek above the dam like we talked about all winter. Maybe we can shoot some film of a mink I've seen along the shore, and maybe we can catch a few fish."

I knew a spot with a large rock that had an isolated, deep hole below that always held panfish.

"I'll take the canoe, and we can put in above the lake where Little Pine enters. There is a small gravel parking lot there, but we'll have to carry the canoe down the hill to the water."

We had discussed it many times while tying flies the past few months and were already pretty clear with what we wanted to do. The warmth of the weather that day brought all those ideas and conversations together into a plan.

We both got together what we needed for the trip, and I knew what gear I had to find for the canoe. It wasn't more than twenty minutes before I had all my fishing equipment gathered in one spot: rod, reel, net, creel, flies, boots, and of course, all the cameras and lenses. I had the canoe paddles, but I searched everywhere and could not find the two life jackets.

"Where could they be? I always had the life jackets!"

We looked and looked and labored over what to do since I had always worn life jackets in colder water. Our plans were so vivid, and since we had gone over the idea so many times before, it seemed only a small point compared to the rest of what we had gotten together that the vests weren't there. The canoe was guaranteed to float after capsizing, so we thought that if we had a problem and ended up in the water, we'd just hold onto the gunnels and swim the canoe to shore. The water was not big in the creek above the lake, and that gave us an extra sense of security. It did not even seem like winter with the warmer temperatures, blue skies, and our plans themselves helped produce the feeling of spring and security.

As we drove south on Route 220 to the exit for 44, just past Jersey Shore, it was still early afternoon, and all those thoughts we had visualized were coming closer to being a reality. We drove north on Route 44 along Pine Creek, and the wide valley was reassuringly bathed in golden sunlight. We got to Waterville and turned right just over the bridge and started along Little Pine Creek Road. We had only ridden a short distance when the narrow, shadowed valley gave us more than a hint that the spring day was different in the small Little Pine Valley. It was darker and held only a glimmer of the distant, sporadic sun. Here, snow and cold hit us with a feeling that the sunny day may not be everywhere. Even with the change in scenery, pent-up excitement still built as we came out of the woods, past Happy Acres and the Little Pine State Park entrance, and finally crested the hill at the top of Little Pine Dam. The view at the top of the hill at the dam made us feel as if we walked into a stone wall! The scene was the opposite of the vision that had played out in our minds. Our spring fever was hit with a sobering reality. Little Pine Lake was frozen, and the seemingly limitless pine forest beyond was still a frozen green and white expanse of ice and snow. Our thoughts turned to hope that Little Pine Creek above the lake would be clear of ice and our plan might still work. Our conversation was a little quieter as we pulled into the small parking area, well past the ice-covered lake; it overlooked a wilder section where the creek flowed along a steep bank before spreading out and creating Little Pine Creek Reservoir. The other side of the creek opposite the steep bank was a series of small islands and snowy hilltops sticking out of the swollen water, with the opposite side partially frozen in backwater snow/ice ponds all the way to the mountain. We parked, got out, and walked to the edge of the bank, overlooking the edge of the creek above where Little Pine Lake was formed. It looked calm enough there in the moving water before it entered the iced-over lake. But we wanted to canoe the creek, and to us, it appeared doable.

We started to unload and carefully carried the canoe down the bank to the edge, just north of where a small tributary enters from the woods above the lake. It was a good spot to launch. Below, the lake was still frozen, but above, the water was much wider, quieter, and seemed to easily flow to the ice below. It didn't appear as if it would be a difficult passage for us to make it to the other side of Little Pine along the small islands sticking out from the water. In later spring, summer, and fall, these islands would have been a part of dry lands, separating the creek from the backwater; the water next to them would have only been inches deep. In hindsight, all this should have been a very clear danger warning. It seems at times that perspective is severely damaged by dreams, plans, and excitement; it creates a different reality from what would be formed by objective thought.

We unloaded the car of our beloved fly tackle, cameras, lenses, and carefully moved back down the hill to load the canoe. We put our camera straps around our necks. We thought they would somehow be safer and able to be used faster by having them right at hand. We both loved photography and took pictures, or actually Kodachrome slides, to accompany the stories we wrote for outdoor magazines. The camera and fishing equipment were another part of the dream to photograph mink along the stream and possibly catch a few very early-season crappies and sunnies. It was well planned and all thought out. We've all heard of a dream come true; and this, we thought, was the beginning of a midwinter dream come true.

Dan stepped into the front of the canoe, and after he was seated, I lowered myself into the back and we pushed off across the quiet inlet through the bottom of the creek above where it entered the lake. We headed for the other shore since our destination was farther up Little Pine Creek to a spot a few hundred yards above our launch point. That plan would put us opposite a few shoreside boulders that had deeper holes downstream of them, which usually held the fish.

The area was also near the location where dark mink were known to prowl and would be the target of our long lenses. It was also along a stretch where the opposite bank was mostly a steep cliff.

We paddled only a short distance when the canoe was hit by a sudden crosswind that came up the lake across the ice; it rocked not only the canoe but our sense of safety as well. We paused with more than a little fear; it was closer to fright! I grabbed the gunnels with tight grips, looked up, and Dan was also stone-still and gripping the sides of the canoe. We both responded to the power of the wind against our craft. I believe that was the moment when our feeling of powerlessness hit. The canoe didn't just get blasted by the wind. It seemed to be twisted as it shivered along its length, a physical reaction from one end to the other like it was flexible, pliable, and very vulnerable. We were headed to a snowy bank on the other side of the current. Below us, spread out frozen in the distance, was Little Pine State Park Lake, and beyond the bank, in front of us, was a wide backwater of ice with the white, snow-laden mountain looming behind. Above, of course, was the blue sky which earlier had given us each that strong dose of spring fever and security.

"Keep paddling," I said, being as reassuring as possible. "We can slowly paddle along the other shore."

As we dug in parallel to the low, white bank rising out of the dark water, we certainly didn't think it was quite as springlike as we had before we started the trip. We moved carefully along, both of us deciding to leave our fishing gear on the bottom of the canoe and our cameras around our necks. Since the incident with the wind, we quickly changed our plans. We thought we could paddle along the other side for forty or fifty yards, turn forty-five degrees downstream, move swiftly to the other side, and follow the bank to where we put in. We both, deep inside, wished we were on the roadside of the creek and safe once again!

We made it farther upstream; but by now, there was a roar to our left from the broken, rushing water in the middle of the creek. Little Pine wasn't so little anymore. On the other side was a high cliff with the road above. The water, I realized, was much larger than

I had ever seen, and it looked much wilder than the friendly small creek it was when I had been there in the past.

"Let's paddle a little farther then angle the canoe down the current at forty-five degrees and shoot for the other side. We'll land farther downstream with this current, but that should put us close to where we started!"

We wanted to get to our put-in (and take-out) spot well above the ice covering the lake. It seemed like a great idea with the current helping to move us across and downstream to where we began. We both agreed and were relieved we had what we thought was a good, cogent plan to get back to safety.

We dug our paddles into the water, Dan from the front and me from the rear. We turned and shot across, moving with the angle we wanted. Our immediate speed in the current was much faster than we had expected. Where we started at the beginning of the trip, we crossed at the relatively peaceful intersection of the stream and lake. It was flat water, and at that point, it widened out into the top end of the frozen lake. This was very different. There was another sense of relief as we got turned and started into the current with enough sunlight left to still feel like we had a good plan and would make it to the other shore. We had told each other at the beginning of the trip, and once again before crossing, that if we flipped, we could hold onto the canoe because it was guaranteed not to sink since it had built-in floatation. We lurched with the helping current toward safety.

Then, as if running into a brick wall, we jerked to a stop. Just as the wind had shaken the canoe earlier, we now again had no control. It happened in less than an instant. The canoe pivoted broadside to the current, perpendicular to the bank, and in the same moment, we flipped and were thrown into the air and into the water upstream. We didn't fall out of a tipping canoe; with force, we were thrown upstream! The fast current pushing into the side of the quickly overturning canoe actually propelled us into the air and into the water and into a new reality from the previous second.

Startling, shocking, and alarming with the loudest blaring sirens, shock, panic, and an avalanche of emotions flooded in from being submerged in the frigid, dark February winter ice water.

Get your head above water and take a breath was the first thought I remember having. *Grab the canoe. You have your hip boots on. Swim. Don't sink!* were thoughts that jumped out as well.

I was thrown up current and came back to the edge of the upside-down canoe. I was startled by having the hip boots on since my father had always told me when I was young that I would drown if I fell in the creek wearing hip boots, that they would fill with water, sink me, and I'd drown.

What goes through your mind in milliseconds—and it seems in slow motion—during an accident is incredible. I kept my feet up as I tried to swim, and the boots actually trapped the air in the lower section and gave me some buoyancy; they helped me get to the surface and swim or crawl or be washed against the side of the bottom of the stuck-in-place, upside-down canoe. I grabbed the side edge of the canoe and threw one leg up onto the smooth bottom (which was now just below the top of the water's surface with water surging over it), and I carefully climbed and slid up onto the surface. Water was flowing over the fiberglass bottom, and it was very slippery. I crawled up, so I was totally on the surface, but it was even more slippery than I had thought, and I had nowhere to hold on.

"Dan," I hollered as I saw my friend grabbing for the rope fastened to the front of the canoe.

The sound of the water was deafening, and the roar only added to the feeling of uncontrollable, cascading, rushing events. Dan had been thrown into the water at the front of the canoe, and by the time he got to the surface, he only had seconds before the current was pushing him around the front. I saw him reaching out to get a hold, but the water was moving him swiftly downstream below the canoe and away from what we thought was our safety. He missed grabbing the rope and was struggling to swim!

I slid back into the water, thinking I could hold onto the gunnel as I put my boot under the canoe to find whatever was holding it in place in the current. My plan was to pull from one end of the canoe to dislodge it, coast to Dan downstream, so we could both ride the floating canoe to shore, holding onto the gunnels. I didn't feel the cold or think of added danger. Ideas just sped from one to another and gave me a rushing list of thoughts and options. I remember thinking it was odd that as I held onto the canoe's edge, I couldn't feel anything with my boots but a strong current under the canoe, just moving depth. I pulled on the very end of the canoe with all my might while being in water over my head. Nothing would budge! Immediately, the deep, watery cavern under the canoe made me understand even more that we were both on the border of life and death.

I crawled back onto the bottom of the canoe, flat on my stomach so I wouldn't slide off. I realized then that the canoe was not going to come loose and we were not going to hold onto it while coasting to shore. I spotted Dan. He was swimming toward the snow-covered bank we had just canoed along.

I hollered, "Swim, Dan, swim."

He was very close to the bank. That was when it hit me that he had on ankle-high winter boots that were laced up and tied. Another thought that flashed in my memory was a story Dan had told me that winter. He revealed an experience about a time when he was fishing a small tributary to Pine Creek that had a thick over-canopy of trees that kept the water very cold all summer. He had spotted where a good-sized trout should be and moved slowly into position to cast. The flat rocks in the stream in the summer were as slippery as an object could be without being ice. As Dan moved, he slipped and went over backward into about four feet of water. He told me the cold had almost knocked him out, that he was lucky he made it out of the water. When he slid onto his back into that stream, he had taken in a mouthful of frigid water and was shocked by his response. He rolled back to his knees and emerged, coughing and thinking he was lucky to have made it. He was astounded that the cold water could be so paralyzing. I automatically prayed that Dan's response to that slip underwater in years past would be totally different today!

The thoughts that shoot into your mind you can't control! And mine at that moment as Dan swam, knowing the canoe was immovable, was to help by hollering to my friend.

"Keep swimming. You're almost there!"

I believed the communication would help keep us both conscious and working in a controlled, logical manner to shore. It is completely incredible what goes through the mind—so many thoughts! I still had my hip boots on with my wet clothes and camera; and in a flat-out position, I clung to the overturned wet bottom of the fiberglass canoe.

Dan was doing well, and it appeared he was only a few feet from the sloping, snow-covered bank when he stopped swimming and he seemed to try to stand. I believe to this day that he stopped swimming because he thought he was close enough to the bank that he could just stand up and walk out. I don't think he was more than three or four feet from the snowbank, which was the water's edge. I thought he had made it, too, as I got renewed confidence that he would soon be onshore. Then, instead of being waist- or chest-deep or so, he went under—totally under. The water depth next to that bank was over Dan's head, and instead of walking a few steps out of the water, he was submerged once again! He thrust his head above the surface, sputtering, coughing, and shouting. I screamed as loudly as I could to redirect his actions, and it was as if I said nothing. His arms thrashed in the water, his head twisted from side to side, and his cries filled our small valley. I see it and hear it still today, and the scene can be so vivid at night. He continued as he slowly disappeared below the surface, into the water over his head but only feet from the snowy bank and life.

The next feeling that overcame me was probably one reason why this story was so difficult to put onto paper year after year and even after so many years. I tried so many times to write what happened, but it never came out the way I needed it to be!

When Dan sank below the surface, still alive and struggling, I was in shock. I was frozen in time and in disbelief. I didn't think the present was real yet. I had thought that other events would occur—that Dan would come shooting up, that certainly he could not be gone, that his life could not have ended in that instant. He could not be gone forever with no other possibility for life. *His life was gone. He was gone.*

"Dan, Dan," I shouted. All was still, quiet, and very cold.

I continued, expecting him to emerge and climb out. I knew he would break the surface and be next to the bank! Everything he was, everything he stood for—his future, his students, his classroom, his baseball team, his kids in the future, the hopes, the dreams, the pride in what he stood for—told me it couldn't be. He was so very connected to life, his parents, his brother, Dan's fiancée! How? There in the graying, frigid gloom seemed nothing but lack of life, only death! It was as if I had been in the worst nightmare, one from which I wouldn't wake. And the gray and cold was growing.

I heard a car where I knew the road was on the other side of Little Pine, above the cliff. It stopped. I could hear the motor, but it was no longer moving. I heard two doors slam and the voices of a male and female; it was as if they were right across the creek. I couldn't see them since the pines were thick from my position. In front of me was the raging water with the soft, green pines above. What a dichotomy of conditions!

"Isn't it beautiful?" one of them said. The other agreed with an interjection describing the ice, snow, and the seemingly velvety green. Sightseers!

I screamed, "Help! Help! Down here! Help, my friend has drowned! Help!"

I don't know how many times I hollered at the top of my lungs. Then I simply heard the car doors shut and the sound of the vehicle slowly disappearing. I was positive at that moment that they didn't hear me because I was struggling to shout over the top of the sounds of the creek's rushing rapids, whereas I heard their voices clearly since it was only against the eerie quiet of the woods above. My feelings raced from a leaping chance that they would hear me and get help to devastation.

Completely alone, I knew I had to swim the same way Dan had swum, and he was such a strong athlete.

Get out of your heavy, waterlogged clothes to give yourself a better chance of making it to shore, I thought. The first thing to go was my 35mm German camera in its brown leather case. I cut the strap with the pocketknife I had brought along and, without ceremony, threw it into the current. Material possessions are completely worthless when your being is condensed to immediate life and death. I started to pull the velour sweater I had worn over my head, but I slipped and almost slid from the canoe bottom. Each action seemed to present a new danger and produced ideas of what had to be done quickly. Since I had been in the water and soaked for probably ten minutes, I somehow knew my time to be physically capable of swimming to shore was decreasing because I was wet and so cold. The late afternoon air was turning even more frigid; time was not on my side.

First, I pulled my velour sweater back down. Nothing would go over my head again! All I needed was to slip back into the water with my arms stuck over my head, tangled in my wet sweater. Carefully, I tugged out of the hip boots and left my socks on, thinking they would give me a little protection from the ice. With the knife firmly gripped in my fist, I felt like it gave me some added advantage. I cut out of the pullover, cut my pants off above the knees, and threw the last vestiges of what seemed like warmth and home to the current. It didn't matter at that time that there were miles of water, ice, and snow to struggle through before I made it back to civilization on the other side of the creek. I knew I had to make it out of Little Pine Creek and up that snowbank first; the rest did not matter if that didn't happen!

I remember it like it is still happening to me. The water was getting higher and higher on my ankles as I clung to the slippery fiberglass bottom. I felt more trepidation as the current from the day's snowmelt was increasing around me as the creek rose. I knew I had to jump in almost immediately or I'd just fall in and die. I also thought and felt as though I was getting stiff; the cold seemed to be settling all the way to my bones. No one would know my thoughts, the struggle that life is worth, and that the gift we have of life is worth everything. It was my last chance.

From so young an age, around three years old, my mother was bedridden for months and we were alone in our half-double house. Dad was working; and my brother, Michael, wasn't born yet, which was the reason Mom had to stay in bed with her difficult pregnancy. I would ask her to play with me or give me ideas of what I could do. Mom was so tired and seemed half asleep.

She would always say, "Just go pray."

I heard this so many times. I had prayed with my parents and had been taught to pray from my earliest recollection, so that was usually exactly what I did.

A lot of kids that age had pretend friends when they were alone. My Friend wasn't a pretend one! He was very real, and I met Him when I prayed! I started this extra praying for maybe a week by kneeling. That position was very uncomfortable after only a bit of conversation, even at three years old, and I started lying flat on the floor on my stomach with my arms spread out. That worked, and with only an occasional change of arm position, I can remember so many great visits in prayer. Bedtime prayers were a lot different. There was a form, a distinct beginning—the Lord's Prayer, then God blesses, and thank-yous. I didn't like these nighttime prayers as much since they seemed like I was just saying something before going to sleep, kind of like summarizing what we believed God did for us, then saying good night. I loved the prayers in the late morning and afternoon; they were my visit and conversation with the real person I studied about with a neighbor, Mrs. Shempp. In her Good News Club, she would present on a flannel board (with refreshments afterward) well-known biblical stories from the New Testament. Mrs. Shempp was great and held the attention of all of us after-school elementary kids. She brought the characters of the Bible to everyday life. She made the stories become a part of who we were and what life was about. My prayers were conversations with the person we studied and sang about with Mrs. Shempp and in Sunday school. They were the best visits with my Friend. He was always there and never too busy to be approached.

My prayer that February day in the water on the canoe as a twenty-four-year-old was much like the conversations I had as a three-year-old. A prayer? Yes. A conversation? Definitely. And it was always two-sided. I knew I didn't have much time. Most likely, my life would be ending soon, and I didn't want that to happen without a fight or without one more conversation.

With my arms spread and raised, I said, "Dear God"—what does one say at such a time!—"well, here I am again. Thank You for being with me. Thank You for sending Jesus to us. You know I need You every day. You already know all that. You also know that I come to You every day to say thank you and to get a new start. I'm saying all this now because I really need Your help. My friend just died, and I have to follow his swimming. I know it is wrong to try to bargain, but please give me a chance to say what I'm thinking. If You help get me out of this, I will still be a very flawed human, but I will come to You daily for help as I usually do. The thing that I can promise is that if You help me live, I will continue to be a pain in the neck to some I work with in my fight for the kids that I teach. You know that has been the case so far, and I will not stop fighting for them as long as I live. If it is Your will, dear God, please help me get out of here. If it is not Your will, please put someone in my classroom who will fight for the needs of my students."

I then asked for understanding and peace for my parents, Mike (my brother), grandparents, relatives, friends, and "kids." I named each of them and pictured their faces as the warmth of their lives flooded my mind. I would miss them! Then it was time for the thank-yous that had never stopped since those early child-hood years.

"Thank You, God, for…" And I went through the special hap-penings with close relatives and the gifts we had shared in our lives. "And thank You God for the needles that fall from the pines and lie at their bases, that warm, beautiful, rusty-brown reposed in thick blankets against their trunks. Thank You for the blue sky, for the rain, for the shapes of clouds, and for the song of birds and peepers. Thank You for the plants, the flowers, the weeds, the hoot of an owl at night, the fish, the clean water, the animals, and (at that moment I had a vivid memory of) the honeysuckle and its wonderful, sweet fragrance. Thank You for our lives and for the energy to act and for our brains to understand what needs to be done to make this world a better, more giving, more loving place for everyone. And most of all, dear God, thank You for You. Thank You for all of Your creation, its beauty, bounty, and infinite gifts of grace we don't even begin to grasp. We are not conscious of or begin to understand its infinite beauty. Thank You for my life and the chance to do Your will and to act to make a difference. Dear God, please give me the strength to get out of here! Please, please be with me!"

I moved to the back of the canoe, which was pointing toward the snow-covered bank, and knew it was past time to swim. The swift water was now acting as if there were no canoe blocking its path, and I dove in with a shallow dive and began swimming and stroking. All my actions seemed to be disjointed. I knew I had to swim, and I knew how to swim, but my arms and legs were not following my directions. It took determination to keep going, not to mention trying to do it in a coordinated manner. The cold penetrated me, movement was agonizingly slow in the swift current, and I couldn't see anything but frigid, dark water. I knew my arms and legs were not moving correctly; I was too slow! It was such a challenge just to move! Then, there was no water, no cold, no thought, only an awareness.

The freezing water, the snow-covered bank, the roaring sounds of the rushing creek, even the cascading and ever-exploding lists of thoughts that had rushed through my consciousness disappeared. I wasn't aware that all my world disappeared; but it did, completely, from my mind. I was connected to nothing in thought of either a physical or a mental nature nor to my present, external world. My existence now was a vivid scene where my grandfather and I were fishing and he was laughing while I reeled in a trout; it was a replay of a very special moment from my early childhood with my grandfather; it was as if I were there again. I felt all the love for PopPop as well as the excitement in catching the fish and the pride I had that my grandfather enjoyed the moment as much as I did. I saw my brother, Mike, lying in his crib when he was only weeks old, and the same thoughts I had at that time of so much fun we would share in life came rushing through. The scene automatically switched from one special moment to another special moment as most of my favorite times with loved ones were replayed; it was as if it were an episode out of the old television program *This Is Your Life*. The last scene triggered sensations of joy, warmth, love, contentment, and family as the four of us—Mom, Dad, Mike, and I—sat on the brown corduroy couch in our old living room. Mike and I sat, listening with wonder as Mom read from *Hiawatha*. I really felt exactly like I was there! It was a feeling of warmth and love. Then, it all disappeared; and I was encompassed in complete darkness, nothingness, a total void or blackness. In the center of the void, a vivid scene appeared. I saw myself lying in a casket, motionless and reposed in the wooden box. The only visible part was my body and part of the casket. There was utter stillness—no life, no sound, no thought. To my left, from the center of the black void, the smallest of embers appeared. It was as if a sparkler were being lit from the smallest of matches. From that pinpoint of light, the ember spread, and it looked like the center of a giant sparkler. The glowing white core of light grew and grew in size. My body, the casket, and the void disappeared, and all that had been in darkness was completely encompassed, transformed, and engulfed by the bright, all-consuming light.

Immediately, the light became my world. Then I opened my eyes. I felt an arm around me, holding me. I can still see what I saw then, as clearly as if it were happening now. I was being held above the water, and I was acutely aware that a hand was pressed to my stomach and was pushing hard. There was a pain in my throat as it and my lungs felt like they were being turned inside out. It was as if I were watching myself as I regurgitated a stream of water that rushed from my throat and open mouth and arched to the creek below. I can still, to this day, see that stream of water coming from my mouth, and I can feel the reflex of my muscles as the frigid column was expelled from inside of me. My lungs hurt. I felt like I was turned inside out as the last water emptied from them.

A voice I can still hear said, "Now swim. It is by My power. Keep swimming."

I was placed back into the water and immediately began to stroke. Now I was able to swim where I had been so slow before.

As I did, I hollered, "Swim," with each stroke and continually told myself to shout "Swim" and to not stop until my hand hit the snow on the bank.

I remember well the moment when the swimming action of the palm of my left hand slammed down onto the top of the bank where there was a rock under the snow surface. I will never forget the feel of that rock! I was onshore!

"Dear God, thank You, thank You!" I hollered and screamed to the hills.

I was completely aware of my surroundings only now and was once again filled with joy for my deliverance from the water and was at the same time filled with horror and remorse for Dan. My socks had come off during the swim, and I stood on that mound of snow in my bare feet, cut-off pants, and white T-shirt, trying to determine what to do next. *Get to the mountain,* I thought, *and work your way up,* where I knew a small woods trail ran along the wilderness side of Little Pine Lake; that path would take me to the top of the dam and eventually to the road on the other side.

I started into the wide, iced-over backwater that existed from my position, all the way to the mountain. One step at a time, but I could only go a few steps and thought, *You can't swim again.* The ice was thin, and I kept breaking it with my feet as I moved forward, but I didn't know how deep the stretch would get, and breaking the ice with bare feet hurt. I just couldn't get halfway across only to turn back! And I couldn't swim again! So I turned back immediately and felt safer when I got back to my original crawl-out spot on the stream's edge. From hiking the area a few years before, I knew there was a field farther up the creek and believed it extended to the mountain. The field started well below the old stone bridge pillar much farther upstream and could get me near the trail without being in water again.

It was a long trudge through the snow, along the creek to the field. My mind seemed to be working clearly, and I wanted to get back to the trail before dark. My feet hurt from the icy snow, but I knew as long as they hurt, they were alive.

"Dear God, thank You for feet!"

The length of the hike to the field didn't matter in my mind because I was out of the water and I was on the way. It was reassuring. Besides, I thought, *I still have the pocket knife I had used to cut the strap of my camera and slice out of my clothes!*

Step after step, the ridge widened but still had back channels between myself and the mountain. That was okay since I was getting farther away from the creek and getting closer to the mountainside.

As I walked, I noticed blood in my footprints. I did stop to massage my feet and had the thought that the circulation would keep them alive and get me back. When I rubbed them, I did notice pieces of flesh missing from the center of the bottom of both feet as well as on the bottom of one big toe. It wasn't hard to know where the blood was coming from. Sitting on an old log, I cut two strips, one from each of my pant legs that were now above my knees. The strips were fastened to each foot, in hopes of protecting the bottoms of my feet. After a few steps, they came loose and slipped away. I abandoned hope of saving my feet. I knew I just could not take any more time from my hike back. It was time to just put all my energy into getting onto the mountain, finding the trail, and moving to the dam and the road beyond.

At the edge of the field, where the mountain rose at a good angle, I found another channel of water, probably from snowmelt on the exposed hillside. It was amazing how devastating that was. I just didn't want anything to do with water again! I walked along the channel downstream and found an old deadfall log. Perfect! It didn't have many branches to stop me from crawling across and was a good width which allowed a tight grip. Crawling and snaking across, it seemed a brief relief for my feet as I kept them elevated behind me. After a few minutes of careful maneuvering, I got off the log and made it to the mountain. One step, then another, and movement!

With a quick glance at an angle up the hill, I saw several deer grouped together, and they were stone-still as they stared at me. What a surprise and sight I must have been to them, especially at that time of the year in that location and just before dark. I thought, *Get the knife out. Maybe, just maybe, you could get close enough to harvest one of the deer.* All I could think of was getting warmth from the carcass and from the fur. I had to get close enough to one to use my pocket knife. I have to say again: what thoughts go through the mind! I moved toward the animals, not easy with the feel and elasticity gone from my feet. I got off-balance and fell, plunged, and rolled to the bottom of the hill. Well, I landed back where I had started, near the end of the log. I took inventory of my condition and realized I was okay, except I had lost the knife in the fall. It was a loss of an item that had given me a sense of security as if I might have a lifesaving use for it in order to get back.

I would have to tell myself several more times on the struggle back, "Stick to the prime directive. Get to where you are going. Stick to the plan."

But each diversion at that time felt like the added thought would help me get through my struggle back. I remember those deer as clearly as that day, but it was probably lifesaving that I didn't think any more of pursuing their fur or their warmth!

Instead of moving far up the slope, this time, I moved along the edge above the channel. It was hard going since it was still a slope and the feeling in my feet was totally gone. Another fact that was disturbing was that there was no longer any blood in the tracks my feet were making in the snow. I hoped my feet would work at least long enough to get me back! I kept moving as steadily as possible toward a hollow between the mountains where I believed one of two small streams entered the lake. I knew that on the other side of the hollow, on the second mountain well above the lake, was where I'd find the old woods trail which paralleled the lake.

The hill got steeper as it approached the hollow, and the hollow was a struggle to climb in the snow. I basically crawled over the knob, through the hollow, and to the side of the woods. The snow was wet and packed under my hands, knees, and feet. The packing made it sharper as it created small, glassy mounds against my skin. In at least my mind, it hurt! After another climb, I saw the line through the trees that was the trail through the woods above and along Little Pine Lake. I was exhausted, and light was turning to a soft gray that made the trees less distinct in the woods. Next to the trail were pine trees, and I noticed that at each trunk where the raised ground met the bark were dried pine needles. The red-brown texture of color added warmth and a remembrance of the beauty nature seems always ready to provide. It was just those pine needles and scenes like that, that I had thanked God for while still on the canoe. I walked a few more feet on the trail and just had to stop for a break. I felt so tired, possibly from traversing the hollow and climbing to the trail. Maybe I was worn out from the struggle, from knowing Dan didn't make it, and from being continuously aware that I wasn't back yet. I had to get back before dark!

I simply lay down in the snow, so happy to be at the beginning of the woods trail, and I just wanted to take a short break. The snow felt soft and warm. It was so wonderful just to lie down for a few moments. I extended my arms and pulled the snow up into a pillow. I was so comfortable. I was just taking a break. *So warm.* I allowed my eyes to slowly close. *It would be only for a short time. So warm.* It felt so good. It was so comfortable. It felt warm, and the break from the fight to survive and protect my feet was a wonderful feeling. I slowly closed my eyes only for a few seconds. *It would be okay. I wouldn't go to sleep.* I faded into what might have been. Then...

There was a loud, watery sound from the upper lake below my position, and it stunned me back to attention. The sound bolted me back from being warm, content, sleeping, and fading into semiconscious comfort. I realized I was no longer aware of the level of my freezing! My mind snapped to consciousness.

You've been given a gift. Dan did not have this opportunity. Don't waste it, my inner voice commanded, and I rose.

It was like I jumped to attention and felt like the race was on once again. I somehow got an extra boost of energy! Adrenaline? *Get back to the objective. Get to the dam and back to the road!* I couldn't feel my feet at all, and walking was now like trudging along on stilts. There was only a peg at the bottom of each leg. I had to keep my balance, but my feet didn't seem to be there and also wouldn't bend. I got started on the trail and found myself beginning to run. As I went, the running seemed to turn into large strides or leaps and gave me the feeling I was going in slow motion. I felt like I was covering large chunks of ground fast. The leaping strides through the woods were something I had never experienced before. It was exhilarating. It felt unbelievable—such long strides, bounding from one point to another. Then my vision started to blur, and the color in my vision started taking on a yellowing hue. In my chest, my heart was pounding like a bass drum! The sound and pounding were almost deafening!

Stop running. You are going to pass out, I thought.

18

I stopped and breathed deeply. My heart began slowing, and the deep breaths helped. The normal color of the graying woods returned, and I felt more secure that I was going to remain conscious. I didn't run again.

There was a small snowmelt runoff not far in front of me—the mind never stops thinking of all the possibilities—and I went to the small flow of water cascading down the forested hillside, put my hands to the bottom, removed a few rocks, and found mud underneath. Perfect. I buried my feet as I massaged them to help them with whatever life and mileage they might have left. I noticed the snowmelt water did not feel cold, even to my hands. My feet had no feeling to the water at all. I knew my time was running out! I massaged my feet and thought, *That's enough. You've got to get back.*

I stepped from the water; *it couldn't be too far from the dam breast.* Now, I walked slowly but with determination, one step at a time. I tried not to think of my deteriorating physical condition except to keep moving while not putting pressure on for speed. I wanted to remain conscious. With the lack of feeling gone from my feet and ankles, it felt like I was now walking on the bottoms of my leg bones. Ahead, the trees began thinning, and I saw more open space. It was where the trail opened to a sloping field just before the dam. Hard not to run when you feel yourself getting closer and the road is across the dam! I would make it to the road no matter what!

The open area was flatter, and keeping my balance was easier if I didn't think of my feet, Dan, freezing, or my deterioration. I took a look at the bottom of each foot, and a lot of the flesh and meat was missing.

"Thank You, God, for feet and for what they do for us!"

Another short climb and I was on top of the Little Pine State Park Dam. I walked eight or ten steps before a new sound made me cringe. The breast of the dam was windblown, and the path across the top to the road on the other side was scattered with small sharp stones—stones that would be nothing to hinder boots or sneakers but stones that ripped and tore at each frozen bare foot. The sound on my flesh was difficult to bear. Along the edges of the areas of stone were dead and matted grass and weed debris. I wove my way across the dam breast, trying to stay away from the sharp obstacles. From time to time, I crawled because it was a lot easier. When I crawled, I didn't have to see the frozen flesh of my feet left on the pebble-strewn dam breast. Either way, the sight of the other side of the dam finally came along with my first sight of the road. That last one hundred feet with my first glimpse of the coming of the road was a gift I'll never forget.

The blacktop was bare, and I moved to the middle of the road. I took stock of my appearance and wouldn't have been surprised if someone had refused to pick me up: limping along, no socks; wet pants cut off above the knees; wet, tattered white T-shirt that had turned a grimy gray; and longish, ratted-up wet hair. It is still hard to believe but I realized I still had on my wire-rimmed glasses (probably because they had the sides that went around the ear). Since I was blind without my glasses, still having them, I was sure, was much more than just another factor that helped save my life.

It was the end of February. *Why would someone like me be standing in the middle of a road, looking like I did? Would someone stop? I would soon find out.* There was the sound of a car coming up the road not far away. Here they were, coming. I raised my arms and waved from the center of the road; they would have to get well off the highway to go around me. They slowed down, so I figured I wasn't going to get hit. They stopped. A father was driving and a boy, possibly a teenager, was riding in the front seat.

I walked to the car and said, "Please take me back to Happy Acres. My friend is dead. He drowned. I need help!"

Happy Acres's store and campground was the direction they had come from and was only a few hundred yards back down the road. It is still, to this day, a private store, restaurant, and campground next to the Little Pine State Park.

I simply grabbed the handle of the back door, jumped in, and said to the bewildered older man, "Please just back up to the store. You can just let me out and take off. Please!"

I collapsed onto the back seat, and we did back up pretty fast and backed into Happy Acres's parking lot.

The dad said, "Let him out and get back in."

I was slumped on my side, and when the son pulled the door open, I fell out onto the fine stones of the lot next to the gas pumps.

"Get back in!" the dad hollered to his son, this time with some agitation.

I can still feel those stones hitting me from head to toe as the driver spun his tires, getting out of the lot. I lay there, but the sound of the car leaving brought people rushing outside from the store.

As it turned out, a snowmobile club was holding a meeting inside the store and hurried to help. The door opened, and they ran to me with pained looks on their faces, not knowing what the problem might be.

"We had a canoe accident. My friend is dead, he drowned, and I walked back here."

They never hesitated as they each carefully grabbed me, lifted, and carried me to a seat behind the counter in the store. As soon as I was inside, they wanted to know where and what happened, with all the details. As I started responding, the store owner had a friend draw cold water from the spigot to put my feet into and got me into dry clothes. When they saw the bottom of my feet, they looked at each other with very pained looks. They all rushed around getting the water, calling an ambulance, helping me out of the wet clothes and into dry ones, and opening chocolate candy bars to provide me with some warmth and energy. I was wrapped in an incredibly soft blanket as I started to tell them what had happened.

Before we started, they arrived with the water.

Lowering my feet, I immediately responded, "No! It's too hot. It hurts."

The person with the water said it was cold water.

Charlie Rohrer, the owner, said, "Go outside and get water from the creek."

As they did, he told me they would slowly add warmer water and lightly massage my feet to get the circulation going. As I started to warm up, I got uncontrollable shivers and shook as if I were still along the stream in wet clothes; the shakes never happened until I was safe, dry, and warm inside the store! To this day, I still think about Charlie Rohrer and his group of friends in the snowmobile club. They were completely caring, giving, and provided exactly what I needed at that moment.

"I can't tell you exactly where it happened, but I think I can pinpoint the spot where we flipped, where Dan drowned, and the location of the hike back by starting at where we put in."

The group listened carefully as I described the top of the lake at the base of the creek and the wide, open spot we traversed. I told them about the wind and that we made it to the other bank with the frozen backwater beyond, that we traveled along the other snowy bank for quite a distance before deciding to angle across with the current, and I told them where we flipped over and where Dan drowned. I described my swim and where I had hit the snow with the palm of my left hand. I showed them the spot on my hand where it hit. It was very personal for me, and I will never forget when the snow crunched down and I hit that rock! Then, I went into the hike back and told them they should be able to follow my footprints from the other side of the dam over the open area, through the woods on the woods trail, over the hollow, down the slope, across the tree, and I told them the way I had gone from there back to Little Pine and down to the site of the accident.

While I was telling them what had happened, they put my feet into a new, large bucket filled with creek water and began adding the warmer water as my feet were carefully massaged. They told me the ambulance was on the way. As soon as I finished, most of the group ran outside. I could hear their snow machine motors start, and they headed across the dam for the woods trail. While they were gone, Charlie fed me again and again. I think I drank ten mugs of hot tea; it felt so soothing. I could feel the warmth go all the way down! Charlie was also very reassuring about my condition but didn't say anything about my feet, which was not surprising because they were a mess. But they got me back!

Still revolving around in my mind were all the scenes from the accident—Dan's swim, the cold, the ice, the snow, and the prayer and being lifted up while the water shot from my mouth. I would think of those integral parts of the accident and my life almost daily for the next forty-five years until the how of writing this finally came into focus. I had begun this story, as the kids I taught would say, *so* many times; but the focus and slant were not at all what they needed to be. Now, I hope I'm getting it right!

It didn't seem long before the sounds of the snowmobiles approaching came back into focus.

The door opened quickly, and one of the guys said, "The boys are following the trail and trying to get to where your friend might be. We found your tracks and followed them to the melt-off stream. After that, the tracks were very far apart. How did you make them? They may have been ten feet or more apart with nothing in between!"

I thought about the questions and appreciated that they verified what I thought had occurred.

"That melt-off water was where I took a break because I thought I was going to pass out. I had been running, and it felt like it was all in slow motion, and I was taking ten-foot strides. It happened just after I had taken a break and I started to slowly run and increased my speed. I had so much adrenalin. I never had an experience like that before," I said.

The man speaking said he never saw anything like it but that, that was what it looked like to him as well. While the rest of the men were working their way back to the creek, he and his friend thought they would ask about my footprints and maybe get more information to pinpoint where the accident happened. Outside, the gray had turned to dark gray and was quickly sliding to black. They were having trouble picking up the tracks around the water I had to go through or over, like the channel with the log. They left again, and before they returned, the ambulance came. I thought about the snowmobilers on their sleds, working their way back to the lake trail. I could visualize them on their trek. It wouldn't be easy even on their machines. I hoped everyone would be safe! What wonderful people!

The EMTs spread out the gurney from the ambulance and started to help me onto the bed.

I saw the buckle straps and said, "I'll do anything you want, but no one will strap me down ever!"

The emergency people were wonderful. They helped me lie down, adjusted the pillow, covered me, and assured me they wouldn't buckle me down; but they did fasten the straps loosely in case of an accident. They simply did everything possible to make me feel safe, secure, and that I was in competent hands. They were everything I could ask for. They did just what I needed in my condition to make me feel safe. Charlie Rohrer and the rest of the snowmobile club wished me well. Each shook my hand or gave me a hug as we loaded for the trip to the Jersey Shore Hospital. I'll also never forget the tea, the peanut butter cups, the peppermint patties, and the genuine caring of that group of people.

The trip down was almost a blur as the technician talked quietly and softly and assured me I would do well, which was amazingly comforting! Not having to be strapped tightly onto the gurney in the ambulance was reassuring, and the calm demeanor of the technician at my side somehow reinforced caring and warmth instead of freezing and fright. That was my external self, that part of me reacting to my present location and company driving down Route 44 to Jersey Shore. It was that part that was still needing safety. But my inside was still screaming for Dan to swim. *Keep going, Dan. Dan, swim, swim, swim!*

Inside, I was fighting my way back from the accident, being comfortable falling asleep on the snow; it was knowing there were only minutes left until what fight was left in me was slowly dissipating while unconsciously freezing, being caressed by snow, surrounded by the graying light, and miles yet to go. My mind was content with the idea that my feet may be beyond repair; at the same time, I felt joy that they served the ultimate purpose in getting me through the woods and across the dam to the road and Happy Acres. Dan was a constant thought and presence, a disbelief, and a fright of what was real and what had just happened.

We pulled into the emergency entrance, and the attendant said, "Now we can get you fixed up."

What a great response! He never stopped being a comfort. The driver also drove smoothly and assuredly along the winding Pine Creek road, along the cliffs, and through that black February night.

The nurses and doctors in the ER were warm and so friendly! I was treated like a longtime friend. Their caring and demeanor took away so much of my trepidation. The nurses were encouraging, the surgeons confident, and they had my complete attention.

I told them, "You can take my feet if you have to. They have been wonderful and got me back."

They started to work immediately, giving most of their bustling action to my feet. One female nurse asked what hot drink I would like.

"Hot tea, please," I said.

They were all unbelievably helping and caring.

"You can take my feet if you have to," I repeated. "They were wonderful and got me through the water and snow, back to civilization. I couldn't ask for more," I said as I tried to reassure the staff.

I saw them look at each other many times, particularly in the beginning. They did give me shots in the arm and shots in the feet. I didn't feel any of them. They took my vitals several times. Probably what bothered me most was the cutting sound the scissors made when the surgeon cut the dead skin and tissue from the bottom of my feet. I wondered how much could be left. He said he was almost done when I commented, all the while I was drinking tea and having a wonderful peanut butter sandwich; the simple things were of the most value! What great people! They were all completely on the side of life—caring, loving, accepting. It was the side that got me through the water, the snow, along the trail, and across the dam to Happy Acres; and they had taken care of me all the way to the hospital. There were quiet times as I lay there, which were actually a constant consciousness of Dan and utter tragedy. Many times that night, I related the sequence of what had happened, and no retelling could erase that it was true, that it was a fact, and that my best friend and his life were gone. His parents would suffer so. They would need to know what was happening right away. Dan's fiancée, who was buying her wedding dress just as we had the accident, would need to be contacted as soon as possible.

Mom and Dad walked into the ER treatment room and gave me hugs. They were relieved to see me, but I also detected some reluctance. There wasn't much left of me. I was still in survival mode, and it seemed at that time that I needed just what the hospital staff had provided—warmth, help, and acceptance. Almost immediately, questions started from my mother about what we were doing. Why were we in a canoe in February? What happened? I started the story again but felt like nothing I said would be acceptable. What mistakes were made, and…and? I don't know…and? I did know the feelings I was getting from my mother, and in many ways, it made me feel I was alone, wet, isolated, and back in the snow-laden struggle. I was happy to be in the hospital with such wonderful people working on me, but waging a war on my inside was the part of me still on the canoe pleading with Dan and trying to get the canoe unstuck. It was knowing my chances of making it back were slim and my life, as well as survival time, was ticking away.

The police were there, and I told them as best as I could where Dan had gone down and how they might get to that spot, both from the boat launch and by crossing the dam and walking upstream through the woods. They had questions centered around finding Dan, and I tried to be as specific as possible. I believe it was my mother who called Dan's parents and it was his mother who got in contact with Dan's fiancée. When Mom got back from the phone call, she was white. It was probably one of the hardest calls she had ever made!

They kept working on me, bandaging my feet and giving me food and hot drinks.

"Well, you are not going to lose your feet," the surgeon said. "It will be a long recovery as the tissue and circulation regenerate. I'm painting the openings in the middle of your feet and your big toes with purple tincture, which will stimulate regrowth. You'll need to keep your feet up as the circulation, tissue, and muscles are recovering. Stay off your feet, and when you can't, use the crutches! You are a very lucky and tough young man."

I answered by telling the whole staff how wonderful they were, both in helping my feet and my need for warmth but also in giving me what I needed, outside and inside. Their skills and attitude helped give me the strength to begin the rest of my life.

And the rest of my life started right then! My uncle Mike, my mother's older brother who was a lawyer, drove my parents to the hospital from Williamsport since they didn't think they were in any emotional condition to drive. When I left the hospital in a wheel-chair, they helped me maneuver into the back seat with my parents as my uncle drove. It was only a few blocks, and we were on the highway; that's when it started. Believe me, there wasn't much left of myself to keep going, but somehow, the energy came.

My uncle said, "So now, with what happened, I am sure you understand that there are important things in life and you get them with what you do with your time. I understand you want to teach, but that isn't going to get you where you should go in life or get you what you want. Go back to school, get your law degree, be a lawyer. I told you there was a place for you in the firm! Stop this philosophical stuff. Your parents didn't raise a dummy."

Now I was totally, humanly alone again. I was facing what I had faced so many times when I was younger. God was with me before in my struggle to survive. He was the reason I did survive, and the prayer on the canoe, together with being lifted from the water, gave me new energy.

I responded with, "You know, my ultimate concern is not money. It has never been money, and it never will be money!"

"I thought this accident may have taught you something," he said.

I answered immediately, "It did teach me something. My friend is dead, his life is gone, and all the money in the world can't bring him back. His life was so much more than a paycheck. It was the kids he taught, cared for, comforted, taught baseball and fly tying to, and made a difference in all their lives. To so many of them, Dan was like a father. He was so much more than what we consider a typical human. He brought bountiful grace to so many where it had been scarce or unknown. My joy is also with teaching and my students. God has let me live, and teaching and fighting for my students are what I'm going to do. Money is at the bottom of my list of wants!"

Mom said, "David," as if I may change my mind and that I should not contradict my uncle (and godfather).

Dad touched her arm silently saying, *Let him alone.*

The rest of the ride was in silence. People didn't talk the way I did to my uncle. I guess by that time I had been used to doing just that. Many great discussions (arguments) had taken place over the years at all family get-togethers. That was one of the places I began learning who I was and what ideals I was willing to fight for. I owe my parents a great debt for providing the freedom of discussion. That night, my parents wanted to take me to their house to stay; but I needed to go to my apartment and start grieving, healing, praying, and doing the adjusting process by myself. They took me into my home and made sure I had everything I needed. I thanked my parents and uncle for picking me up, and they left. I collapsed on the couch.

I was out of school for the next few weeks, but in the meantime, life was busy not only in my mind but with a few friends, relatives, and regular visits from the state police. I spent a lot of time on the couch, watching the fish and insects in my fish tanks and putting on record albums. The bottoms of my feet were a constant throbbing, and I used music to distract my thoughts from the pain. I was alone most of the time, so the music I listened to was therapeutic in my mind. There were so many thoughts. There was so much internal pain, so many questions echoed to edge out the distracting words of my favorite music. Some albums did help. When I felt completely down and had no energy, I tended to listen to Neil Young or the Moody Blues. They were not a disguise from being depressed. They had their own downers which made me face my feelings. They were like friends who understood where I was in my mind. It really helped me through the bottom times. I had transition music that, when I was ready, took me from the lows to a more thoughtful, contemplating condition. This was fulfilled when listening to and singing along with Carole King and Bob Dylan. It was like they were there and their words spoke to me! When I was able to feel much more positive and needed a stronger, more constructive partner, I listened to Simon and Garfunkel as well as Peter, Paul, and Mary. These artists always provided the messages of the ideals of my generation. I think these groups helped make me what I was. When I needed the energy to make it through tasks at hand, whether it was visitors, police, or just eating, I tended to move on to Santana or the Stones; they usually simply gave me energy. Who couldn't listen to the Stones and feel ready for almost anything? There were others, but they tended to be favorite songs from the Temptations, Grateful Dead, the Who, and the Beatles. I only bring this up because they filled a lot of very lonely, isolated, questioning times! They still produce incredible thoughts, memories, and emotions!

I guess I was surprised how quickly the state police came to interview me the next morning after just getting home Sunday when my uncle and parents picked me up at the hospital. The police were incredibly friendly and treated me carefully as if I were fragile. I imagine that was very cognizant of them. I'm sure I was much more fragile than even I understood. I greatly appreciated their demeanor. They were much like the medical staff at the hospital and Charlie Rohrer and the snowmobile club at Happy Acres; it helped me beyond expression!

I hobbled to the living room door to answer the bell, and a uniformed officer was there. We said our hellos and he came in.

"I have a few questions concerning the accident," he started.

"Did they find Dan yet?" I asked before the officer could really get started.

"No," he said. "I thought if I can jog your memory, it would help us in our search. I'd like as much detail as you can tell me about what happened."

I started with the conversation about canoeing, fishing, and filming that Dan and I had the day before—Saturday, February 27, 1971—that we'd get the gear together and I'd pick Dan up at his house. I told him about the search for the life jackets and the conversation afterward about whether we should go or not. The telling got even harder after I had told it so many times. The officer just kept taking notes and let me continue. I followed with the launch of the canoe above the lake, the shaking in the wind halfway across, the fright, the moving along the snowbank on the other side of the creek, and the decision to turn quickly and angle to the other side. Filling in all the detail, I told him about flipping and being thrown upstream, about being washed back to the canoe with Dan being washed around the front end and grabbing for the rope and my trying to work the canoe loose as Dan swam. I kept telling the story about hollering for Dan to swim after I thought he'd made it; he was only feet away from the shore. My telling included as real as possible my total disbelief and sense of loss and defeat when Dan disappeared below the cold surface. Then, my telling centered around the cutting out of my clothes, the prayer, seeing my past and myself in the casket, the darkness, the light and being raised from the water, the stream of water gushing from my mouth, the voice telling me to swim and that it was not by my power. The rest I gave chronologically as my struggle had unfolded. The officer did not react; he only took notes. I ended with praise for those who were so helpful, caring, and loving.

He closed his notebook and said either he or someone else would be back. He thanked me and asked me to call if I had any other facts that might help. He said there would probably be others who'd want to talk to me concerning the investigation. Before he left, he turned back around and asked if I'd be willing to go back to Little Pine to help if they still couldn't find Dan.

"How would I get there?" was all I could think to ask.

The officer said they would pick me up in a cruiser and bring me back.

"Sure," I said. "If that would help, I would be happy to do it. I can't drive or even move around very well though. I think I can tell you where I believe he will still be."

He thanked me again and left.

So many great people was all I could think! After the officer, it seemed like I had a long day with a lot of thoughts—periods of utter disbelief would consume me. The thought of Dan still somewhere there under the water in the current, alone, made me feel like I was still there as well with all the same thoughts I had in that cold, cutting, battering water and snow.

My parents came and brought dinner as they did many of the nights until I could walk better with the crutches. It was so appreciated, but it was hard at the same time as I could tell they were really grieving for the loss of Dan and for the Maustellers. I think my parents were also suffering because of what almost happened to their elder son. To say it was difficult is an incredible understatement.

I told them I thought we just need to appreciate life and love one another—simplistic yet all-consuming! It was to me!

One hour, one day, hundreds of thoughts converged into a stream that I had to control and make sense of. An officer did come back Monday and asked if I could be ready for the cruiser to pick me up to go back to Little Pine Dam. I don't remember much about the trip up Route 220 or Route 44 along Pine Creek. I think that was filled with hope, that I could help, and anxiety about the process. Also, I concentrated on not having the pain in my feet consume my ability to help. I tried to keep them elevated on the rear seat of the car. If they were elevated, there was less pain. If they were down, the pain was consuming. We pulled into the upper portion of Little Pine Creek State Park, and I was dumbfounded by the scene. Cars were everywhere, the afternoon sun was bright, and a lot of the snow had melted on the southern-facing, grassy slopes and had groups of people picnicking. It was like a summer day and completely disjointed from the purpose of what was happening. People noticed that I was in the back of the police car and started gathering outside, getting close to the window for a better view, and, believe it or not, they were taking pictures. An officer came over and moved the sightseers away from the car. All I could think of was how the scene was such a very strange dichotomy between despair, grieving, and exhaustive searches on one side mirrored by an afternoon out with picnic lunch and games on the other. I don't know of a name for what I saw, but if the scene were a word, it would be an *oxymoron*. I guess we as a people are so different in our thoughts and perceptions that such opposite occurrences could be happening at the same time; to me, it was bizarre. In some ways, it put me back in the accident on the canoe, listening to the sightseers on the road above tell each other of such a beautiful scene while I knelt below, wet, freezing, and screaming for help!

There were many boats with search people moving into action, then back to the boat launch. They hadn't yet found Dan but had located the canoe. The weather had warmed so much during the day that a lot of the snow I had trudged through had melted and the water level in the creek as well as in the dam impoundment had really increased.

I told the officer, "If they found the canoe, they can find Dan."

He told me they were afraid the higher water may have moved him into the dam under the ice. I didn't think so since the water closer to shore, even if it is deeper, would be much slower. It was not around a bend or in a place that channeled the current toward the bank. In the cruiser, several searchers, officers, and I talked about where Dan should be in relation to the canoe. "He should be thirty or forty yards below the canoe and closer to the eastern or wilderness shore." I couldn't understand why they hadn't located him yet since they had found the canoe!

They left, and another officer opened my back door and told me Dan's mother would like to talk with me. She was also in a cruiser two cars over.

"Yes," I quickly said.

He helped me out onto my feet, and I made it to Mrs. Mausteller.

"Come here, come here," she said as she opened the door with her welcoming arms wide open.

"Oh my love, my love," she said. "My God, my God," she repeated as she enveloped me with her arms and her love. "What you have gone through…"

It was an incredible response to seeing me and being with me! What love she still had within her to give. She had just lost her first-born son. They hadn't found him yet, and she was providing me with much-needed nourishment for both my body and my soul. I will never forget Dan's mother. We sat there in the back of the cruiser—hugging, talking, and sharing our feelings and what we were going through.

Mrs. Mausteller told me Dan's uncle had gone to Little Pine Dam the night of the accident and retraced my steps across the dam through the woods, across the field, and downstream, back to the water in the vicinity of the accident. He hollered for hours, hoping Dan had made it out of the water and needed help making it out of the woods and snow. He called and walked in all directions, hoping that somehow Dan had crawled out. I felt so awful for him. He wanted so much for Dan to have survived. His disbelief, like mine, was total. You had to know Dan to understand he was rock solid. He brought so much to life! We all just had to go on.

I told Dan's mom what had happened in an abbreviated way; some details would only have hurt. She held me as I talked, and the officer in the front seat was very quiet. She felt so bad as I retold the events. I felt so bad to tell her what happened, but she wanted to know. When I was finished, the car was very quiet. I asked if I could come and see her from time to time. She said her husband wasn't in a condition for visitors right then but maybe later. I understood. I told her how sorry I was that we had taken the chance to canoe that day on the creek. I told her what an incredible friend Dan had been and how wonderful her son had been to everyone who knew him. She actually smiled and told me she knew.

She said, "He is with God now."

I believed that for sure!

Most of the people watching the search had left by the time the afternoon light started to fade. The officers told us we should also leave, and we loaded into the cruisers that brought us. What a terrible trip home it was. My feelings for Dan, the Maustellers, and his fiancée consumed me; and there was no outlet, nothing more that I could do!

It wasn't long after the trooper dropped me off that the phone rang and the police told me they found Dan.

"Where did you find him?" I asked.

"Dan was close to where you thought he'd be. There were several more feet of water than when you were there. The current was more swift and off color since the water had come up since the accident. It took two motorboats to dislodge the canoe," the officer explained.

He also told me my father had picked up the canoe.

"Thank you so much for letting me know and for everything you and the other officers have done," I said, and we hung up.

I had a sense of peace that Dan had been found, although it was weighed against so many thoughts and emotions on the other side. I could only feel for Dan and his family.

It was a very long Monday in so many different ways. I was so relieved they found Dan. I was also very relieved and happy to have talked with Mrs. Mausteller, and it felt good to have helped with the search, even in a small way, and I had gotten through the day physically. Everyone was such a help! The next few days until Thursday's viewing left me completely unsure of what I should do.

I did know by then that recovery was far from easy and wouldn't happen until sometime in the future, and even then, it would never be complete. This became especially clear the first time I stepped into the bathtub to shower. My feet were covered above the ankles to protect the open sores and stitches, so I felt it was okay to finally step under the shower. The water temperature was perfect, so I slowly moved forward and stepped under. *No!* My mind reacted immediately. It knocked my breath away. *Get away from the water.* Panic hit me just as if I had been catapulted back into the creek. I felt, in the second that I got under the water, that I couldn't breathe, and that the water was completely consuming me once again. It was like I was totally in Little Pine again and unable to breathe! What a fright! I jumped back from the shower, wiped the water from my face, and felt immediate relief to be out from under the water streaming over my head. I felt like I could breathe again. I didn't try to rethink what was happening at the moment. I stepped out of the tub, turned the shower off, and felt immediate relief. I'll never forget that panic and the feeling of the water consuming me. It was such a comforting feeling to turn the shower off! I used a washcloth and got decently clean again. It did take a while and many experiences with my bathtub to regain the ability to be secure in getting under the water again, even in the shower, to complete what had always been a normal routine. It felt great when this routine could be completed without trauma!

While my body very slowly healed, especially my feet, I was also trying to get myself back to the feeling of a more normal functioning mode. I knew that in a few days, Dan's viewing was going to be held. What shall I do? I guess I was still in survival mode at that time, much more than I would have ever admitted. And it probably was a pretty good idea. I did as much as I could from the couch because I was trying to give the circulation and tissue on the bottom of my feet a chance to get started to rejuvenate and heal.

I remember the doctor told me, "Stay off your feet and keep them elevated."

I listened to music, played my acoustic guitar, read a little, and thought all the time. Those thoughts were grueling. I am sure you can imagine what those thoughts were. The accident, death, freezing, wetness, cold, struggle, staying conscious, getting back—it was all-consuming much of the time. I did pray, not only every day but quite a few times throughout the day. The prayers were as they usually had been throughout my life, and many times, it was hard to tell when I was praying and when God was simply a part of my consciousness. Don't you think throughout the day, no matter what you are doing, if you think about it, you realize part of your thoughts include God? That is not much different from prayer, or not different at all unless you compare the conversation and thoughts to a more formal, memorized prayer. Even the formal prayer can be a good place to begin with as it is familiar and can be a good introduction to a conversation with the Lord. They were my days leading up to the viewing.

There was a snowstorm as the day approached, and there was over a foot of snow in town with much more in outlying areas. It once again brought into sharp contrast the extremes that can occur from day to day and what effect time has on human plans. I decided to go to the viewing, and I am still glad I did. I had incredible trepidation as I approached the door. I would see Dan again, and I would see many others that his death impacted. Of course, I wanted to go to say goodbye to Dan and, somehow, to say it in person. "I am sorry this happened to you, my friend!" I knew for sure it would be very difficult to be there, but I felt it was what I needed to do.

I reached for the doorknob, and the door opened. The attendant welcomed me and took my coat. I looked across the area, through the inner archway, and there was Dan! I started with the crutches to move toward my friend when a doorway opened to the side from another room where family and friends could gather and grieve; then it seemed as if a whirlwind of people were rushing in. I was shaky to begin with, but with the group rushing to and into me, I ended up in a pile on the floor amid a lot of confusion. There were a lot of tears, a lot of loud words, and a lot of raw feelings that were released in those moments as I tried to get back up off the floor. I felt so bad for everyone. I was sure that seeing me brought back as many thoughts and feelings for the others as seeing Dan did for me. The other people moved off as Mrs. Mausteller helped me get back up. I slowly moved to Dan and stood there. I said nothing out loud, but my thoughts were as if I were speaking. *I am so sorry, my friend. We should have made other choices when we saw the scene at Little Pine Lake, but our plans and dreams were great. If we had made it, our experience would have meant so much. I am just so sorry! Be assured I will fight for the kids we both taught, and you and your wonderful accomplishments for the kids will never be forgotten.*

Life was not there as I looked at Dan, but the shell of the friend who was so great was a reminder of how magnificent a gift our lives are and that we must use it every day to the fullest as Dan had done. I drank in the presence of Dan, of all he had been, and thanked God for my friendship with him. I thanked God for all Dan had accomplished, and I prayed for all his school kids and family. I looked at Dan one last time, at his coat and shirt and tie, then I saw the Orvis jumping trout tie tack. That detail stood for Dan! I smiled at him and his wonderful jumping trout and memories of all the flies he had tied and the brook trout he had caught on his favorite run, and I remembered the great Mausteller Mayfly Nymph he had invented. I walked to the door, got help with my coat, hugged Mrs. Mausteller once again, and left into the snow and the night.

There was so much snow. They didn't bury Dan for several weeks. Everything came to a standstill. Life for me was no different except it didn't come to a standstill; it was already at a standstill. I was only trying to understand. I guess I was attempting to grasp the meaning of what happened by thinking of everyday life. I should have gone back to my childhood and my mother's advice, "Just go pray." What her advice had done was to allow me to escape the everyday happenings and needs and connect me to the Spirit, which is alive and within each of us.

Still, in my head, I was trying to put myself back into the life I had before the accident. And I attempted to regain who I had been in my mind before that February day. I found it was impossible to again be who I had been! I was no longer the same person. Who I was had its foundation built on precepts from my earliest of ages. I was changed and molded from the understandings derived through a continuity of events and new understandings that occurred singularly to me as life went on. I was always open to change. I found change to be exciting and not a small part of what it meant to be alive and grasping the future. This is about as far as I got in understanding before it was time to go back to the classroom.

I was still on the couch most of the time with my feet elevated, so I knew going back would not be physically easy. When I stood for just a short time, the bottoms of my feet throbbed and felt like a hot poker was below each arch. The doctor told me to keep them up on another chair once I was in my classroom. They were still completely wrapped, and I was still on crutches, so not much weight was applied to the injured bottoms. Actually, I was so happy just to still have my feet.

The day finally came, and I got a ride to school. We pulled up across the street where the front door of the school was visible and only a short walk from the car. I got help to the front door, and my ride left. Opening the door gave me a feeling that I was returning to the old self I had been trying to recover. The biggest difference here was that I was so excited to see my students! The rest I was not quite so sure of.

The walk up the steps to the second-floor office where teachers signed in was slow and painful but full of hope as my mind worked off the memories of what my students and I had accomplished. We had so many plans and dreams we knew we could achieve in the months ahead! I turned to the right at the top of the steps and opened the door to the office.

Most of the teachers were around the counter and gathered behind—a typical morning. I moved to the counter to sign in, and to me, the conversations seemed to subside. I immediately had the same feelings I had at the funeral home when the people rushed out of the side room. Emotions and personal thoughts poured out from some of the faculty. It was particularly hard for those who were aware that Dan's fiancée had just picked out her wedding dress at the same time as the accident. His fiancée was a teacher in another building in the same district, and so many people were aware of the very difficult feelings. I heard the word "murderer," and it was almost as chilling as hitting the ice water when Dan and I flipped over. I knew what I was, and I also understood the emotions others had about the accident and what Dan's fiancée had been going through ever since. It was hard. I knew some were happy to see me and smiled a welcoming look. I lowered my head and left to go to my room.

The steps once again were difficult, and my classroom was on the third floor to the right of the stairwell, right above the office. It was like walking into paradise when I opened the door and moved to my desk. Very soon, my classroom aide was there and brought a chair to elevate my feet. It felt like I was home! The minutes ticked by, the bell rang, and finally, my students came in and gathered around.

"Meeting," I said, and we all gathered around my desk (instead of in a circle around the center of the room like we usually did).

I told them in an abbreviated form what had happened, how I still needed to heal, and what the doctor told me I had to do to keep improving. I also told them how great it was to be back with each of them and how much I had missed them—all of them! I could feel them caring for me as they listened.

And I had missed them. I looked at my students and knew that it was each one of them in their own individual, unique way that gave me the depth of the meaning of my life. As I had sworn to God on the canoe, "I will fight for my students and their needs." Here they were, my students. There was God, and the rest of what I swore I would do was up to me!

Of course, the weeks went by, and we made progress in subject areas, but I thought there was something more I was missing. It came to me while I was thinking of the accident and my own awareness of why our judgment to still continue our canoe trip was off. I thought, *What if my students were able to contemplate what they were composed of individually and react to that by deciding to control their reaction to extraneous stimuli? The beginning of being able to accomplish that would be to relax in a controlled setting, to put the present thoughts and agitations at rest, and simply concentrate with their minds and physical beings, relaxing and going beyond every day, that they would be able to put all the clutter of the mind in a space by itself and enjoy concentration, awareness, and peace.*

My whole class went to the gym, lay on the hardwood floor, and I started telling them a story. I had explained to them in advance what I was going to do and how we were going to go beyond the everyday experience. They and their parents (who I had talked to earlier) thought the idea was cool, and they were all totally sold on giving it a try.

"Stretch your right arm, stretch, stretch more, you are feeling your arm working to stretch, and after a struggle to stretch even more…relax! Stretch your left arm, stretch, stretch more, you are feeling your left arm working hard to stretch…relax!"

We stretched each leg, we stretched the ankles and feet, we moved the head and neck, and we tightened the stomachs. We stretched to the limit and relaxed. When the stretching was completed, I told them that their bodies were relaxed and no longer a distracting factor in dealing with their thoughts or urges, which had made some of them unable to concentrate.

It worked! We did this every afternoon! It worked so well that the students' parents started calling and asked me to record the instructions not for their children but for themselves. They found their kids were going to bed, relaxing, and going to sleep for the first time they could remember, and they wanted to be able to do the same thing.

I decided that since the students began to understand what they wanted from school for themselves and how they wanted to learn, they became an integral part of dealing with attention deficit disorder. When the students, some in particular would feel their concentration was getting difficult, they would raise their hand to go to the bathroom, and I would give permission by waving with a thumbs-up sign. One special student comes to mind that really had to work at completing his assignments. He worked for fifteen to twenty minutes, raised his hand to go to the lavatory, and I gave him a smile and a thumbs-up, which was letting him know we were communicating and that I respected that he was telling me it was time for a break. He left, had a drink outside our room at the water fountain, looked outside the window at the playground, walked around the U shape of the third floor to the lavatory on the other side of the school, went into the bathroom, washed his face, came back, got another drink, and reentered the classroom. He had the smile of a Cheshire cat that just ate the most delicious meal; it was a grin I will never forget. The grin was not that he had gotten away with something; it was that he knew he had controlled his typical reaction to extended concentration and had gone beyond! He had matured, thought, and controlled who he was and ultimately his future.

All the students started to keep track of how long they could concentrate, work, and accomplish what was expected. This was the beginning of each student being conscious of who they were and what they needed to do to get to where they wanted to go. Before this, many times, impulses determined who they were. They were conscious of themselves and their world and its options. After this, all the subject areas were much easier to teach since the students took charge of their responsibilities to learn and complete work. They were aware of who they were, they were conscious of their school world and the possibilities that entailed, and it appeared, they simply woke up! To me, this was all a direct result of the canoe accident and the thinking that occurred both by them and by me since that terrible day.

As it turned out, this accident and consequent awareness and understanding gave me a monumental building block that would definitely stimulate change. This was when the direct impact of Dan's death was greatest on me. I believe it is the accidents or all of our bumps along the way in life that give us the opportunity for new understandings, change, growth, and increased awareness and consciousness to be a part of our lives. If we are more aware and conscious of the changes, we grow and our world expands and we have a new life. My life is now new every day! I would integrate what I now knew what my life was about and what I had said on the canoe to be a reality for the future. The canoe accident was one more step in the formation of myself and my unique, individual consciousness. To me, we each have our unique consciousness from which we are aware of and react with the world outside of ourselves. I firmly believe the more conscious and aware we are, the more attuned we become to the Spirit which is in all of us. Then, we can begin to transcend the trappings of the conventional in everyday life. We can begin to become what we were intended to be. This process is never done; we are always just one step closer to taking the next step. My life is now new every day!

I firmly believe Dan had understood that. He knew that out of college, he could have played professional football or baseball, and he still chose to be a teacher of children who had special needs. He gave up piles of money and accolades to help individuals he cared so much about. But to Dan, he gave up nothing and was the beneficiary of being able to use his gifts to make a better place for other humans. He developed the Mausteller Mayfly. He developed a special baseball league for his students. He loved all those he taught, all those he came in contact with, and he loved his extended family, which included just about everyone. He was a very special human being!

Each of us is very special. Our specialness, uniqueness, and giftedness become clearer as we are more aware of who we are, and we develop a consciousness of how we fit into the world around us and how we can bring this new horizon to those in our world. It is a big world—a beautiful, natural world—and a life that is only waiting for us to see, enjoy, and appreciate. Please, look at the needles that fall from the pines and lie at their bases. See those warm, beautiful rusty-brown needles reposed in thick blankets against their trunks. Drink in the blue sky, feel the rain, know the shapes of clouds, and let your lullaby be the song of birds and peepers. Let into your world plants, flowers, weeds, the hoot of an owl at night, fish, clean water, animals, and honeysuckle with its wonderful, sweet fragrance. Feel and be aware of your lives and the energy to act. Allow your brains to understand what needs to be done to improve our world. Make this world a more giving, more loving place for everyone. Be aware and conscious of all of the creation—its beauty, bounty, and infinite gifts. Be totally aware of your life and the chance to use your gifts to act to make a difference.

I hope this writing helps to unlock for you your own special way to pray and helps you to be conscious of the Spirit within you. I hope it gives you the impetus to know and enjoy and explore each day and to always love yourself, our natural world, and our fellow humankind.

ABOUT THE AUTHOR

This writing has not been an easy undertaking for David. How does one tell of a life-happening event so extreme that, to him, there are few comparable examples? Who was he that this would happen to him?

David taught school for thirty-four years, was an editor of two outdoor magazines, and has countless articles and columns published in numerous magazines and newspapers. It has now been fifty years since that terrible day. He wrote the chronological happenings so many times, but the words never did it justice. The memory of what happened is still fresh for him, as if it just took place. There has been no time since then that David has not thought of the events leading up to the canoe accident and no time since then that he has not tried to understand what happened and the implications for his life. David's telling now postulates no reason for this to have occurred, and it makes no conclusion as to why the outcomes affected Dan and him in such opposite ways.

CPSIA information can be obtained
at www.ICGtesting.com
Printed in the USA
BVHW031224070423
661948BV00002B/331